CONNECTICUT

Christine Webster

Published by Weigl Publishers Inc.
123 South Broad Street, Box 227
Mankato, MN   56002
USA
Web site: http://www.weigl.com

Library of Congress Cataloging-in-Publication Data available upon request from the publisher. Fax: (507) 388-2746 for the attention of the Publishing Records Department.

ISBN 1-930954-89-1

Printed in the United States of America
1 2 3 4 5 6 7 8 9 10   05 04 03 02 01

Editor
Michael Lowry
Copy Editor
Diana Marshall
Designers
Warren Clark
Terry Paulhus
Photo Researcher
Angela Lowen

Photograph Credits
Every reasonable effort has been made to trace ownership and to obtain permission to reprint copyright material. The publishers would be pleased to have any errors or omissions brought to their attention so that they may be corrected in subsequent printings.

Cover: Church (Corbis Corporation), Vegetables (Corel Corporation); **Connecticut Historical Society, Hartford:** pages 13B, 16B, 17T, 17B, 18T, 18B, 19T, 19B; **Connecticut Office of Tourism:** pages 3B, 8T, 13T, 16T, 21T, 23T, 23B, 25T; **Corbis Corporation:** pages 27T, 27B, 28T; **Corel Corporation:** pages 3T, 4T, 10T, 10B, 11T, 11B, 14T, 14B, 21B, 22B, 26T, 28B, 29B; **Digital Stock Corporation:** page 22T; **Digital Vision:** page 15B; **Jack McConnell:** pages 4B, 6T; **John Muldoon/Connecticut Office of Tourism:** pages 3M, 5T, 6B, 7T, 7B, 12T, 12B, 15T, 20T, 25B; **Steve Mulligan Photography:** pages 8B, 9T, 9B; **PhotoDisc Inc.:** pages 26B, 29T; **Photofest:** pages 24T, 24B.

CONTENTS

INTRODUCTION

Connecticut is one of six New England states, located in the northeastern corner of the United States. Despite being the third-smallest state in the country, Connecticut has much to offer. The state is a perfect combination of old and new. It is a place where busy seaports blend into magnificent coastal views and where bustling cities are supported by colonial architecture. In the countryside, autumn leaves provide a vibrant backdrop for the state's many white-steepled churches. Connecticut's beauty is truly breathtaking.

Since Connecticut was the first state to have a written **constitution**, it is not surprising that its official nickname is "The Constitution State." During the 1700s, the Connecticut Yankee **Peddlers** traveled across the country with horse-drawn carts that were filled with various items for sale. The Connecticut Yankee Peddlers were very sly. Some peddlers sold small, wood-carved "nutmegs" in place of real nutmegs. Soon, Connecticut also became known as "The Nutmeg State."

Fruits and vegetables are important crops in Connecticut.

White-steepled churches dot the Connecticut countryside.

QUICK FACTS

Connecticut is one of the original thirteen states. It became the fifth state to enter the Union, on January 9, 1788.

The sperm whale was chosen as Connecticut's official state animal in 1979. During the 1800s, Connecticut was ranked second, only to Massachusetts, in the nation's whaling industry. Whales were caught and used to make lamp oil and other products. Today, the sperm whale is an **endangered** species.

The Merritt Parkway was built in the 1930s. The highway was designed to emphasize the pleasure of driving.

Getting There

Connecticut is the southernmost state in New England. It is bordered by Massachusetts to the north, New York to the west, Long Island Sound to the south, and Rhode Island to the east.

Connecticut is a gateway for highway routes into New England. Vehicles can whisk through the state in less than 3 hours. Connecticut is also within a few hours drive of major cities, such as New York and Boston. Connecticut is linked by an extensive highway system. Among the major highways is Interstate 95, which runs along the Long Island Sound. Interstate 91 is ideal for transportation, as it heads north, all the way through New England and up to Canada.

Connecticut's many airports help connect it to the rest of the world. The Bradley International Airport, located north of Hartford, is the state's major airport. The Metro-North Rail Service carries thousands of passengers each day to New York City and locations across Connecticut.

QUICK FACTS

Connecticut has more than 20,000 miles of highway and more than 600 miles of railroad track.

Native Americans originally named the area of Hartford *Saukiog*. It was renamed Hartford by the colonists in 1636 after Hertford, England.

The curving, tree-lined Merritt Parkway is considered one of the most scenic highways in the nation.

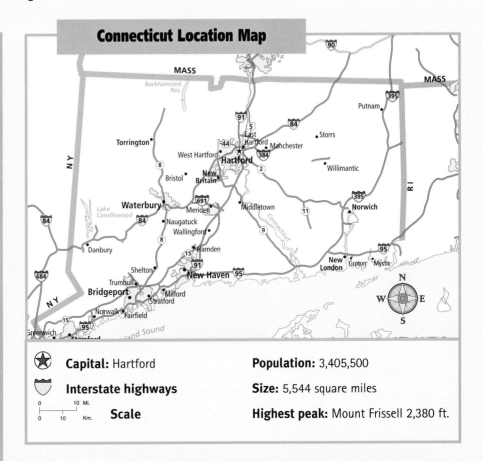

Connecticut Location Map

Capital: Hartford

Interstate highways

Scale

Population: 3,405,500

Size: 5,544 square miles

Highest peak: Mount Frissell 2,380 ft.

There are approximately 4,000 farms in Connecticut.

Connecticut's name comes from the Algonquian word *Quinnehtukqut,* which means "land beside the long tidal river." The broad Connecticut River flows down the center of the state. Its riverbanks were once home to many Native Americans. Early colonists built Connecticut's first towns along the river. Hartford is one of the state's original towns. Ships carried goods from Hartford to locations around the world. Today, Hartford is the state capital.

Connecticut's lack of abundant natural resources forced colonists to use their creativity to invent new products. Since the United States **Patent** Office opened in 1790, Connecticut inventors have filed for more patents than any other state. Many brands of cigars, clocks, combs, firearms, and hats bear the "Made in Connecticut" stamp. During the nineteenth century, Connecticut peddlers sold their inventions throughout the United States.

QUICK FACTS

The state insect is the praying mantis. It was adopted in 1977.

The Capitol was constructed out of marble and granite. It cost $2.5 million to build and was completed in 1879.

In 1987, Carrie Saxon Perry became mayor of Hartford. She was the first African-American woman to be elected mayor of a large city.

The robin was adopted in 1943 as Connecticut's official state bird.

Ships have been built on the Mystic River since the 1600s. More than 600 vessels were constructed on its shores between 1784 and 1919.

Connecticut is the wealthiest state in the nation. It has the highest **per capita income** and one of the lowest unemployment rates in the United States. People are attracted to Connecticut for its excellent employment opportunities. The strength of its economy is a result of the industrial and service sectors, as well as its skilled and educated work force. Many of Connecticut's past inventions are still being manufactured in the state. Factories produce weapons, sewing machines, jet engines, helicopters, motors, hardware, cutlery, clocks, and submarines. The growth in finance, insurance, and real estate contributes to Connecticut's wealth.

This quaint New England state combines its strong economy with excellent educational facilities, pleasant living conditions, rich history, vibrant culture, and beautiful scenery. Connecticut is truly one of the finest states in the country.

Connecticut is home to one of only two shipyards in the United States where submarines are built.

QUICK FACTS

In 1983, the USS *Nautilus* was named the official state ship. It was the world's first **nuclear-powered** submarine, and the first ship to reach the North Pole. It was built in Groton in 1951.

The official state song is "Yankee Doodle." During the American Revolution, soldier Edward Banks wrote the lyrics to this song. While the British soldiers had their own version, Banks created new words to sing back at Britain for poking fun at them.

Picturesque roads lined with giant maples wind through Litchfield Hills.

LAND AND CLIMATE

The Connecticut River divides the Constitution State in half. The Eastern and Western Highlands are on either side of the river. The Connecticut Lowland Valley runs through the center of the highlands.

The Eastern Highlands consist of low, thickly forested hills. This fertile area has few elevations over 1,000 feet and is drained by several rivers. Many hills are level and have been cleared and used for agriculture. The state's highest altitudes are found in the Western Highlands. Thick forests cover much of this rugged area.

The Connecticut Lowland Valley is comprised of reddish sandstone, shale, and deep, rich soil. It is home to Connecticut's best farmland.

Connecticut has a moderate climate with four distinct seasons. Summer temperatures can average 72° Fahrenheit. Winter temperatures range from 24°F in the Taconic Mountains to 30°F in the southeastern part of the state.

Connecticut has 161 square miles of inland water.

QUICK FACTS

The lowest recorded temperature in Connecticut was –32°F on February 16, 1943, in Falls Village. The highest recorded temperature was 106°F on July 15, 1995, in Danbury.

Author Mark Twain once stated, "If you don't like Connecticut weather, wait a minute." Connecticut's weather can change daily from a heat wave to a cold spell, or from a pleasant day to a storm.

Connecticut experiences one or two mild earthquakes each year.

Connecticut's jagged coastline stretches for 253 miles along Long Island Sound, which is an extension of the Atlantic Ocean.

Connecticut is known for its beaches, which are either sandy or rocky.

NATURAL RESOURCES

Water is an important natural resource in Connecticut. It provides energy for the state, habitats for fish, and transportation routes for boats. Until the middle of the nineteenth century, Connecticut's rivers and waterfalls produced much of the state's power. Fast-flowing waterfalls turned the huge waterwheels of factories or mills that were built along the shores of the waters.

While Connecticut was once almost entirely covered by trees, most old forest has since been cut. Forest removal exceeds its growth in Connecticut. Still, Connecticut is one of the country's most heavily wooded states. Its forests range from broad woodlands in the northwest to patches of trees along the southern shoreline. Hardwood trees, such as white oak, American basswood, and hop hornbeam, are valuable to the lumber industry. There are about eighty-five sawmills that process lumber in Connecticut.

During the eighteenth and nineteenth centuries, Connecticut's trees were used for shipbuilding and for fuel.

QUICK FACTS

Connecticut has about 8,400 miles of rivers and streams. Connecticut's three major waterways are the Connecticut, the Thames, and the Housatonic Rivers.

While Connecticut's soil is generally infertile, rich soils can be found in the state's river valleys.

Among Connecticut's most important minerals are limestone, granite, clay, and traprock. Garnet is the official state mineral.

A part of Connecticut is found in New York. Connecticut supplied the granite used for the foundation of the Statue of Liberty.

The scenic waterfalls of Southford Falls State Park showcase Connecticut's natural beauty.

Native Peoples across North America used the bark from birch trees to make canoes.

QUICK FACTS

The majority of Connecticut's woodlands are privately owned.

The white oak is the official state tree. It was adopted, in 1947, in remembrance of the historic Charter Oak. In 1662, Connecticut received a charter from King Charles II, of England, granting land to the residents of New England. Twenty-five years later, King James II sent officials over to New England to retrieve the charter. Joseph Wadsworth hid the charter in an ancient hollow oak tree. The tree was named the Charter Oak. Unfortunately, it was knocked over by a storm in 1856. A monument remains in its place.

Connecticut's maple trees produce 12,000 gallons of syrup each year.

PLANTS AND ANIMALS

Connecticut's beautiful scenery is enhanced by its many plants and trees. The most common types of trees include hickory, oak, maple, ash, white pine, hemlock, red cedar, and other hardwoods.

Common flowering plants are pink dogwood, wild cherry, jack-in-the-pulpit, and the state flower, the mountain laurel. Until the nineteenth century, animals grazing in the fields helped control the spread of poison ivy. Since farming has declined in Connecticut, poison ivy has spread and now consumes many plants.

Connecticut is home to many endangered plants. The balsam fir, the Indian paintbrush, the white milkweed, the hairy lip fern, and the goldenseal are endangered.

The Connecticut Department of Environmental Protection provides many programs that research and protect Connecticut's natural resources. One important program is the **reforestation** of state land.

Azaleas are known as "the royalty of the garden." They can be found in gardens throughout Connecticut.

QUICK FACTS

There are about 50,000 white-tailed deer roaming through the fields and woodlands of Connecticut.

When the first settlers arrived in Connecticut, wild turkeys were very common. Harsh weather, hunting, and the clearing of forests caused the wild turkeys to disappear after the 1800s. By the 1950s, forests had grown back, and wildlife biologists released some wild turkeys in the area. Today, there are between 18,000 and 25,000 wild turkeys throughout the state.

Connecticut has many endangered animals. These include the bald eagle, the bog turtle, the grasshopper sparrow, the leatherback turtle, and the redheaded woodpecker.

Millions of years ago, dinosaurs such as *Dilophosaurus*, a meat-eating dinosaur, and the *Otozoum*, a four-toed dinosaur, were inhabitants of Connecticut. By the time the first European settlers arrived, different kinds of animal life existed. Many deer, wolves, and smaller animals, such as porcupines and foxes, occupied the land. Humans have forced out most of the large animals, like panthers and bears. Today, rabbits, beavers, minks, squirrels, and raccoons inhabit Connecticut. While most birds migrate each year, blue jays, chickadees, and robins live in the state year-round. An occasional visitor to Connecticut is the snowy owl.

The *Dilophosaurus* grew to lengths of 18 feet and was once common in Connecticut.

Connecticut's many streams and lakes are stocked with bass, perch, pickerel, and trout. Oysters, lobsters, and crabs are found along the coast. The Fisheries Division of the Connecticut Department of Environmental Protection manages Connecticut's fish supply. It keeps a close watch on the populations of fish and endangered species. The fish populations are increasing as a result.

Connecticut is home to a number of minks. These animals are extremely agile in water, where they catch fish, frogs, and shellfish to eat.

TOURISM

Connecticut's rustic landscape, sandy beaches, and busy harbors attract millions of visitors each year. Connecticut also offers tourists a glimpse of history. Visitors can take a step back in time as they walk through an old seaport. Located halfway between New York City and Boston, Mystic Seaport offers a rare portrait of maritime life. Visitors can tour a re-created seaport village and board early nineteenth century whaling ships to see how sailors lived 100 years ago. This world-renowned museum occupies three of the five shipyards that once functioned on the Mystic River. More than 600 vessels were launched from this site between 1784 and 1919. Mystic Seaport attracts more than 1 million visitors each year. Other features include the last wooden whaleboat in the United States, a planetarium, and the largest collection of maritime photographs in the world.

The Barnum Museum, in Bridgeport, is a popular destination for circus fans. The museum is a celebration of the life of one-time Connecticut resident P. T. Barnum, creator of "The Greatest Show on Earth." Visitors can learn about the 25-inch, 15-pound Tom Thumb, or Jumbo the 1,500-pound African bull elephant.

William Gillette began construction of his spectacular castle in 1914. The project took 5 years to complete.

The Barnum Festival, held annually in Bridgeport, is a month-long celebration that ends with a Fourth of July parade.

QUICK FACTS

Tourism brings $5 billion each year to Connecticut's economy. Hunters spend more than $40 million per year in the state.

Children can learn about the marine life of Long Island Sound at the Maritime Aquarium in Norwalk. It contains displays of more than 1,000 marine animals. Visitors can catch a closer look at oysters, seahorses, lobsters, and other small creatures or stare into the eyes of a 9-foot shark. Displayed in a 110,000-gallon open ocean tank are sharks, bluefish, and rays.

Located on a cliff high above the Connecticut River, lies the Gillette Castle. Designed by actor William Gillette, the castle is one of Connecticut's most favored attractions.

Fishing boats are common in Connecticut's coastal waters.

Connecticut has a low unemployment rate of about 2 percent.

Very few farms in Connecticut make more than $10,000 per year. As a result, most farmers have a second job. Connecticut farms produce dairy products, eggs, fruits, hay, potatoes, tobacco, and **nursery** stock.

INDUSTRY

Connecticut's economy has changed through the years. While most of the early settlers were farmers, the number of farms rapidly declined as land became scarce. Many farmers went to work in factories, leaving only 4,000 farms in operation by 1999. Connecticut turned its focus toward industry, and manufacturing became one of the leading industries. Today, nearly one-third of the income earned in Connecticut comes from manufacturing.

Shellfish were once abundant in the coastal waters of Connecticut. In the nineteenth century, the annual catch declined due to pollution. Despite this, commercial fishers catch approximately 3,600 tons of seafood, including flounder, cod, and lobster, each year.

High-grade broadleaf tobacco is used to make cigar wrappers. Tobacco growing has been an important industry in Connecticut since the 1830s. It is grown under a permanent cover of open-mesh cloth that is held up by poles. The mesh protects the tobacco from direct sunlight and heavy rain.

By 1810 there were fourteen textile mills in Connecticut.

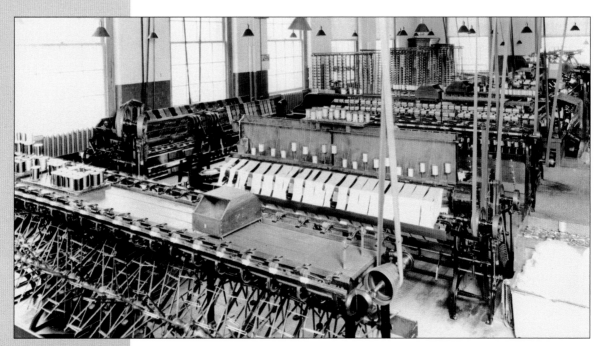

GOODS AND SERVICES

George Smith gave the lollipop its name. He named the candy after a popular racehorse.

Connecticut's lack of abundant natural resources forced its citizens to develop new ways of making money. Creative citizens have developed many important inventions, such as **vulcanized** rubber, steamboats, submarines, and corkscrews. In the 1850s, Isaac Merrit Singer was the first person to develop a sewing machine for commercial use. The Bradley-Smith Company in New Haven first invented the lollipop in 1908.

Approximately 1,692,000 people are employed in Connecticut. Fourteen percent of the work force works in manufacturing. Jet aircraft, computer equipment, transportation equipment, and submarines are manufactured in the state. Pez candy and Lego toys are also made in Connecticut. The state's principal manufacturing centers are Hartford, Bridgeport, New Haven, and Danbury.

QUICK FACTS

In 1982, Dr. Robert K. Jarvik, from Stamford, invented the world's first artificial heart.

More than half of the state's work force is employed in the service industry. Service positions include nurses, teachers, and store clerks.

The state capital, Hartford, is only about 100 miles from New York City or Boston.

Connecticut publishes twenty daily newspapers.

First published in 1764, the *Hartford Courant* is the oldest continuously published newspaper in the United States. Thomas Green started the paper as a weekly and kept it going by selling clothing, hardware, and stationery out of the front window in his office.

The first working helicopter in the Western Hemisphere was designed by Igor Sikorsky of Connecticut in 1939.

Nathan Hale, who was hanged by the British as a spy in 1776, once taught at this schoolhouse in East Haddam.

The insurance industry, along with financial services, generates the most money in Connecticut. The insurance industry was created in 1810 for merchants who were concerned about the protection of their ships. For this reason, the Hartford Fire Insurance Group was formed. It is the nation's oldest insurance company and still operates in Hartford. It is now known as the Hartford Insurance Company. Another large insurance company is Aetna and Travelers. There are 106 insurance companies in Connecticut. Hartford is one of the world's centers for insurance and, as a result, is known as the "Insurance Capital of the World."

Education has always been important in Connecticut. The state's first public school opened in 1641 in New Haven. Today, more than 537,500 students attend the state's 1,178 public schools. Connecticut is also known nationally for its private schools. About 77,000 students attend the state's 350 private schools. Several notable post-secondary schools can also be found in Connecticut. The oldest and most well-known university in the state is Yale University. It was founded in 1701 in New Haven and is the nation's third-oldest university. Other notable schools are the University of Connecticut, Trinity College, and the University of Hartford.

Approximately 85 percent of Connecticut's population has a high school diploma.

QUICK FACTS

Connecticut earned the nickname "The Insurance State" more than 180 years ago. Marine insurance was the first type of insurance available. Ship owners wanted protection for their ships. Merchants were concerned that fires, pirates, storms, or accidents would threaten their trade.

In 1650, a law was passed requiring every town with more than fifty families to build an elementary school. Those towns with more than 100 families had to provide a secondary school as well.

Connecticut has 195 tax-supported libraries. The most important library collection is held at the Yale University Library. It is home to more than 8 million books.

The Mashantucket Pequot Reservation is home to about 115 residents.

Native-American groups often traded with one another before European settlers arrived. A group living near a river may have traded their fish with a group living in a wooded area for deer meat.

The name Pequot comes from the Algonquian word *pekaqatawog* and means "destroyers." The Pequot lived in the eastern part of Connecticut and along the shores of Long Island Sound.

Residents and tourists can still hike the many original trails cut by the earliest Native Americans.

In the 1970s, Native Americans began moving back to the Mashantucket Pequot Reservation, hoping to restore their land, their culture, and their community.

FIRST NATIONS

Thousands of years before the first settlers arrived, Native Americans were living in the Connecticut area. By the 1600s, there were about 7,000 Native Americans. They belonged to several Algonquian-speaking groups. The most powerful of these were the Pequot. They inhabited approximately 250 square miles of land. Other groups included the Mohegan, the Narragansett, and the Saukiog. The Native Americans cut trails through the dense forests to travel between their villages. They would hunt animals and gather wild berries for food. They would also fish in the streams and grow beans, corn, and squash. The Native Americans often traveled with the seasons to take advantage of the natural resources. They built **wigwams** and **longhouses** from saplings, and used bark and branches to cover them.

As Europeans started to arrive and purchase land from the Native Americans, tensions grew into the first major war of New England—the Pequot War of 1637. The colonists formed alliances with the Mohegan and the Narragansett and led a surprise attack on the Pequot, destroying their village. The remaining Pequot were captured and sold into slavery, or held under the control of other Native-American groups. The surviving Pequot became known as the Mashantucket Pequots.

The Algonquin of the eastern woodlands preferred the larger, dome-shaped wigwams to the teepees used by other Native-American groups.

Reverend Thomas Hooker helped found colonies at Windsor and Wethersfield.

EXPLORERS AND MISSIONARIES

Dutch explorer Adriaen Block sailed south on the Connecticut River and along the coast in 1614. He was the first European to reach Connecticut. Native Americans greeted him in peace. Block sent reports back to Europe of the land's beauty and trade possibilities. In 1633, the Dutch set up a small trading fort at the end of the navigable portion of the Connecticut River, near the present site of Hartford. It was called the "House of Hope." The Dutch soon became trading partners with the Native Americans.

Settlers from nearby Massachusetts were also exploring the fertile Connecticut River Valley. They had left their homes in Great Britain in search of political and religious freedom. A group led by Reverend Thomas Hooker left Massachusetts to form a colony in Hartford. About 250 Europeans from Boston bought Connecticut land from the Native Americans. They paid with twenty-four knives, twenty-three coats, twelve spoons, twelve hatchets, some scissors, and a few garden hoes.

QUICK FACTS

Reverend Thomas Hooker encouraged the colony of Connecticut to form a new government. He felt that citizens should be allowed to choose their own leaders.

Animal fat and ashes were used by the colonists to make soap. Each spring, children would sit and stir the soap for hours over an outdoor fire.

From 1790 until 1840, Connecticut's population increased by between 4 and 8 percent every 10 years.

English Puritan settlements began expanding into the Connecticut River Valley in 1633.

Education was important to the early settlers. In 1650, a law was passed requiring every Connecticut town to teach children how to read and write.

EARLY SETTLERS

The state's earliest colonists were farmers. They raised only enough food for their own needs. These early settlers grew vegetables and grains, and kept a few animals. They made their own clothing, tools, and weapons. The forests provided the colonists with wood for fuel and for construction.

In 1638, representatives from Hartford, Windsor, and Wethersfield met to discuss plans to unite the settlements. On January 14, 1639, the Colony of Connecticut was formed. The colonists adopted a basic set of laws. These were written down and were called the Fundamental Orders. This document is one of the first written constitutions in history. A legislative and a judicial party were set up, and John Haynes was chosen as the first governor of the Connecticut colony.

Nathan Hale's last words were, "I only regret that I have but one life to lose for my country."

QUICK FACTS

The Fundamental Orders were a basic set of laws that would create a self-governing colony. Loyalty of the residents would be to Connecticut, not England.

Connecticut is the only state to have an official hero. Nathan Hale was a spy for General George Washington in 1776, but was caught by British soldiers and hanged. Connecticut adopted him as their official hero in 1985, for his courage and determination.

By 1800, 83 percent of Connecticut's African-American population was free from slavery.

By the late 1700s, the population of Connecticut had reached 237,946 people. This was approximately 6 percent of the total population of the United States. While most of the citizens were of European heritage, a few hundred African Americans were brought over to the colony from the south to work as slaves. Settlers from France, Scotland, and Ireland moved to the state and set up jobs as carpenters, tanners, and tailors.

In the mid-1800s, Connecticut outlawed slavery. This gave all African Americans freedom. The 1900s brought in a wave of **immigration** from Europe. Many people had come from Ireland during the great potato famine of 1840. Others, such as Italians, Irish, Germans, Russians, and Canadians, came to Connecticut because of the state's growing demand for labor. They were followed by groups from Sweden, Norway, and Poland.

QUICK FACTS

During the 1700s, many farmers looked forward to visits from traveling peddlers selling small wares, such as hats, pins, buttons, rifles, clocks, and tableware.

Pumpkins were once used to cut hair in New Haven. Cut pumpkins were used as guides to ensure a round and uniform style. New Englanders were nicknamed "pumpkinheads" as a result of this style.

There was a large amount of work to do on early Connecticut farms. Farming families were often large, and every family member had specific chores to do.

POPULATION

Hartford is the second-largest city in Connecticut, with about 139,700 residents.

Although Connecticut is the third-smallest state, it is the twenty-seventh most-populated state in the country. It has a population of about 3.4 million people. This means that there are 677 people for every square mile of land. As a result, Connecticut is the fourth most densely populated state in the nation. Most residents live in urban areas, such as cities. The largest cities are Bridgeport, Hartford, New Haven, Stamford, and Waterbury. Small and sparsely populated towns still exist in the countryside. Many people choose to live in these rural areas for the peace and the quiet they offer.

About 175 Native Americans live on five reservations throughout the state. Two large Pequot reservations can be found in Ledyard Town and North Stonington. A tiny reservation, about one city block in size, is in Trumball. A few Native Americans live on the Schagticoke reservation in Kent.

QUICK FACTS

While Montana is almost thirty times larger than Connecticut, Connecticut has about four times as many people.

The Constitution State has 8 counties, 21 cities, and 169 towns.

Bridgeport is the largest city in Connecticut. It has a population of 141,686 citizens.

The coast of Connecticut is considered the "Gold Coast." Wealthy towns along this coast offer huge homes and marinas filled with luxurious sailboats.

Connecticut Cultural Groups

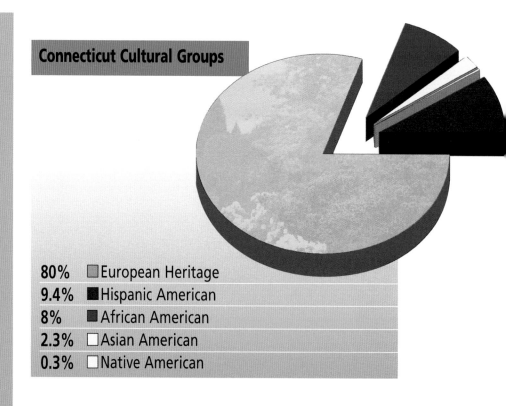

80%	☐ European Heritage
9.4%	■ Hispanic American
8%	■ African American
2.3%	☐ Asian American
0.3%	☐ Native American

POLITICS AND GOVERNMENT

The first meeting in the Connecticut State Capitol was held in January 1879.

Connecticut's earliest settlers created the first constitution. Today, the state is governed under its fourth constitution, which was adopted in 1965.

Connecticut has three branches of government. The governor, who is elected by the people to a 4-year term, heads the executive branch.

The legislative branch consists of a bicameral, or two-house legislation. It has a 36-member Senate and a 151-member House of Representatives. Each is voted to 2-year terms. The legislative branch is responsible for making the laws of Connecticut.

The judicial branch oversees the punishment of those who break the laws. The highest court, the Supreme Court, oversees cases from people who feel their constitutional rights have been **violated**.

Small towns and local governments use a system called "home rule." Each community elects a selectman, or mayor, in the larger towns, who controls issues, such as land use and education.

QUICK FACTS

In 1662, Connecticut had twin capitals, New Haven and Hartford. Hartford became the sole official capital in 1873.

In 1974, Ella Tambussi Grasso became the first woman to be elected as governor of a state without being preceded by her husband. Grasso was also the first Connecticut governor of Italian descent.

The state flag consists of a white shield against an azure blue background. On the shield are three grapevines, while under the shield is the state motto.

The vines on the state flag represent the first English settlements in Connecticut. Founded by settlers who moved from Massachusetts in the 1630s, these settlements were thought of as transplanted grapevines.

Pizza, a traditional Italian dish, is enjoyed at the Festival Italiano.

QUICK FACTS

Roman Catholics are the largest single religious group in Connecticut.

African Americans make up the second-largest cultural group in Connecticut.

African Americans live mostly in the five largest cities of Connecticut. Thirty-five percent of the populations of New Haven and Hartford are African American.

Nearly 630,000 people in Connecticut are of Italian descent.

CULTURAL GROUPS

While most residents of Connecticut were born in the United States, they can trace their roots to ancestors from all over the world. About 90 percent of the population is of European heritage. Within this group, Italian Americans are the most numerous. Italian Americans are proud of their culture and love to demonstrate this each summer, during the Festival Italiano. Every July, several towns in Connecticut hold the festival. It features Italian foods, arts, and crafts. Festival-goers have the opportunity to sample some of the best pizza Connecticut has to offer. The Sons of Italy sponsor the event, and the money raised goes to charities.

New Haven helps the Irish Americans celebrate their ancestry by hosting an annual Saint Patrick's Day Parade. Visitors can dress up in green, listen to live Irish music, watch dancers do a jig, and taste different green foods and drinks. The biggest event is the parade itself, which consists of 1,500 participants and about 500 bands.

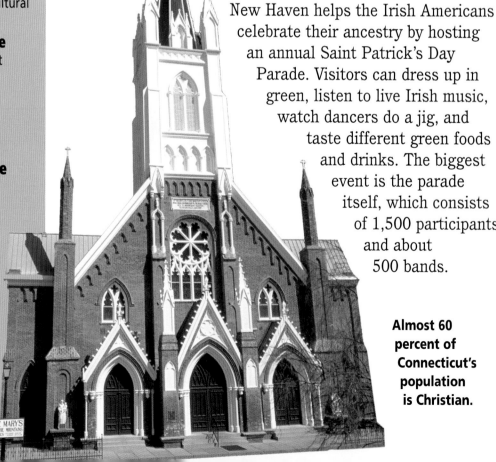

Almost 60 percent of Connecticut's population is Christian.

The Durham Fair is the largest agricultural fair in Connecticut.

Several thousand Native Americans in Connecticut celebrate their culture each year. The Mashantucket Pequot Tribal Nation puts on festivals that showcase their rich traditions. One such festival is the annual Feast of Green Corn and Dance, called the "Schemitzun." More than 3,000 participants compete in the World Dance Championships. Visitors can view more than 100 Native-American craft vendors and watch demonstrations of handwoven baskets. The Mashantucket Pequots also operate Foxwoods, the world's largest casino complex. It brings in about $1 billion each year.

Many other cultural festivals are held in the summer and the fall of each year. The Connecticut Scottish Festival, in Goshen, features bagpipe players and dance competitions each October. While food festivals serve traditional New England food, many have added rich flavors from China, Ireland, Italy, Mexico, and Puerto Rico. Many ethnic restaurants can be found throughout Connecticut.

Native Americans host and participate in powwows throughout the year. These large events showcase Native-American cultural heritage.

ARTS AND ENTERTAINMENT

Mark Twain's real name was Samuel Langhorne Clemens.

Many well-known entertainers and artists hail from the Nutmeg State. Actor Paul Newman studied drama at the Yale Drama School, in New Haven. Newman starred in numerous movies and even owns a food company, called "Newman's Own." Movie star Katherine Hepburn was also born in Connecticut. Hepburn won four Academy Awards for Best Actress throughout her impressive career. Actor Glenn Close was born in Greenwich. She appeared in *101 Dalmations*, playing the evil Cruella DeVille. Children's author and illustrator Maurice Sendak is also from Connecticut. Sendak wrote and illustrated the popular children's book *Where the Wild Things Are*.

One of Connecticut's most-treasured theaters is the Long Wharf Theater. Many plays perform here before moving to larger audiences in New York City. The Shubert Performing Arts Center is considered to be Connecticut's center for cultural life. It has hosted more than 300 world premieres and 50 American premieres. In addition to theater, the center also offers opera, dance, and music performances.

QUICK FACTS

Well-known author Mark Twain had a home in Hartford. It was there that he wrote *The Adventures of Tom Sawyer*, *The Adventures of Huckleberry Finn*, and *The Prince and the Pauper*.

The extremely popular play *A Streetcar Named Desire* made its debut at the Shubert Performing Arts Center.

Many well-known contemporary musicians have homes in Connecticut, including Michael Bolton and Meatloaf.

Glenn Close has been nominated for five Academy Awards.

There are more than 55,000 cataloged specimens in the Yale University dinosaur fossil collection.

One of the best places in the world to see real dinosaur tracks is at Dinosaur State Park. Dinosaur tracks were discovered in Rocky Hill in 1966. Since then, more than 2,000 tracks have been uncovered. The tracks range in length from 10 inches to 16 inches, and are 3.5 feet to 4.5 feet apart. The 200-million-year-old tracks are housed under a giant dome. Visitors can make plaster molds of dinosaur footprints.

Visitors can learn about the history of Connecticut's Native Americans at the Mashantucket Pequot Museum and Research Center. Visitors can walk through a Pequot village set in 1550.

Each summer, Music Mountain hosts the oldest continuous Summer Chamber Music Festival in the United States. It is a pleasure to listen to the beautiful sounds of the Gordon String Quartet. In May, residents can watch the Balloons over Bristol festival. Hundreds of hot-air balloons are launched into the sky, while those on the ground are provided with entertainment, a carnival, and a crafts fair.

The Mashantucket Pequot Museum and Research Center is owned and operated by the Mashantucket Pequot Tribal Nation.

SPORTS

With more than 275 caves and caverns, Connecticut is a spelunker's paradise. Spelunkers are people who explore caves. They have to wear warm clothing and a helmet. They also use light sources, such as flashlights, to see fascinating rock formations or glimpses of animals such as bats.

The state's many forested hills and valleys invite hikers and horseback riders. The Appalachian Trail, which cuts through northwest Connecticut, is a perfect trek for two feet or four. The streams, lakes, and waters of Long Island Sound have popular areas for swimming, boating, camping, or fishing. Fly-fishing is a popular sport in Connecticut.

In the winter, skiers gather at the many hilltops and ski resorts. Mohawk Mountain, a very popular place to ski, is Connecticut's oldest and largest ski area. Other winter activities include ice-boating and ice-skating.

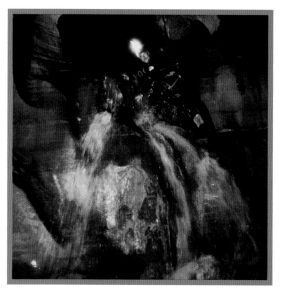

Spelunking is an exciting but risky sport.

QUICK FACTS

Connecticut's first settlers named Kettletown State Park. They bought a 492-acre piece of land from the Native Americans for the price of one brass kettle. As a result, the name Kettletown was given to the area.

Connecticut has ninety-one state parks. Hammonasset Beach State Park is the largest park to border Long Island Sound.

In 1995, Rebecca Lobo, the University of Connecticut's star basketball player, was named the best female college basketball player in the nation.

Skiing is a popular sport in Connecticut among both locals and tourists.

The first Connecticut Huskies basketball game was played in January 1901.

College sports are played all over the state and attract many fans. The University of Connecticut's basketball team, the Connecticut Huskies, has many supporters.

In 1995, Connecticut hosted the Special Olympic Games in New Haven. This event attracted 7,000 athletes, 2,000 coaches, 45,000 volunteers, and 500,000 spectators. It was the largest Special Olympics in sports history.

Latin Americans brought the game of jai alai, a form of handball, to the United States. Jai alai is similar to racquetball, except that players use baskets instead of racquets. The baskets are attached to the player's arms and are used to catch and throw a small hard ball against a wall. Helmets and padding help the players avoid injury caused by the speeding ball. Players begin the game by marching out to a special song, called "España Cani."

The Connecticut Wolves soccer team plays at Veterans Memorial Stadium, which seats 8,848 fans.

QUICK FACTS

Connecticut used to have their own professional hockey team—the Hartford Whalers. This National Hockey League (NHL) team played at the Hartford Civic Center, but after 25 years, the team moved to North Carolina and became the Carolina Hurricanes.

Baseball teams from Connecticut have captured the Little League World Series title four times.

Soccer is a popular sport in Connecticut. The state even has its own professional soccer team—the Connecticut Wolves.

Brain Teasers

1

In 1901, Connecticut passed the first automobile law. What did they set the speed limit at?

a. 10 miles per hour

b. 12 miles per hour

c. 20 miles per hour

Answer: b. The speed limit was set at 12 miles per hour.

STOP

2

When working as a spy, Nathan Hale often disguised himself as a:

a. priest

b. schoolmaster

c. doctor

d. lawyer

Answer: b. Nathan Hale often spied on the British disguised as a schoolmaster.

3

True or False:

Connecticut's state shellfish is the lobster?

Answer: False. Connecticut's state shellfish is the eastern oyster.

4

Who received the first patent ever issued to a woman in the United States?

Answer: Mary Kies of Connecticut received a patent for a machine that weaves silk or straw.

5 Which of these products were invented in Connecticut?

a. frisbee

b. tape measure

c. friction matches

d. nuts and bolts

e. all of the above

Answer: e. All of these products were invented in Connecticut.

6 Who was Connecticut's state governor in 2001?

a. Jeb Bush

b. George E. Pataki

c. Rick Perry

d. John G. Rowland

Answer: d. John G. Rowland was elected in 1995 and re-elected in 1998.

7 **True or False:**

The Connecticut River is the longest river in New England.

Answer: True. The Connecticut River is 407 miles long.

8 **True or False:**

In 1793, Eli Whitney invented the first nuclear submarine.

Answer: False. Eli Whitney invented the cotton gin, which is used to clean the seeds off of cotton.

FOR MORE INFORMATION

Books

Boyle, Doe. *Guide to the Connecticut Shore*. Old Saybrook, Conn.: Globe Pequot Press, 1999.

Collins, Andrew. *Connecticut Handbook*. Emeryville, Cali.: Avilon Travel Publications, 2000.

Squier, Elizabeth. *New England*. Old Saybrook, Conn.: Globe Pequot Press, 1999.

Web Sites

You can also go online and have a look at the following Web sites:

State of Connecticut
http://www.state.ct.us

ConneCT Kids Web site
http://www.kids.state.ct.us

Connecticut Tourism
http://www.tourism.state.ct.us

Dinosaur State Park
http://www.dinosaurstatepark.org

Some Web sites stay current longer than others. To find other Connecticut Web sites, enter search terms such as "Connecticut," "Hartford," "Mystic Seaport," or any other topic you want to research.

GLOSSARY

constitution: the laws and principles under which a government runs a state or country

endangered: in danger of becoming extinct

immigration: the arrival of people in a new country

longhouses: long, one-room dwellings where several Native-American families lived together

nuclear-powered: operated by atomic energy

nursery: a place where young trees or other plants are raised for transplanting, for sale, or for study

patent: an exclusive right granted by the government to an inventor

peddlers: people who travel from place to place selling goods

per capita income: money made per person

reforestation: the planting of trees in a region that has been logged

violated: to break a law, rule, or agreement

vulcanized: rubber treated with sulfur and heat to give it strength

wigwams: round Native-American homes formed by poles and covered in bark

INDEX